The L.A. Riots

Titles in the *American Disasters* series:

The Exxon Valdez
Tragic Oil Spill
ISBN 0-7660-1058-9

Hurricane Andrew
Nature's Rage
ISBN 0-7660-1057-0

The Mighty Midwest Flood
Raging Rivers
ISBN 0-7660-1221-2

The Oklahoma City Bombing
Terror in the Heartland
ISBN 0-7660-1061-9

Plains Outbreak Tornadoes
Killer Twisters
ISBN 0-7660-1059-7

San Francisco Earthquake, 1989
Death and Destruction
ISBN 0-7660-1060-0

The Siege at Waco
Deadly Inferno
ISBN 0-7660-1218-2

TWA Flight 800
Explosion in Midair
ISBN 0-7660-1217-4

The World Trade Center Bombing
Terror in the Towers
ISBN 0-7660-1056-2

The L.A. Riots

Rage in the City of Angels

Michael D. Cole

Enslow Publishers, Inc.

44 Fadem Road   PO Box 38
Box 699   Aldershot
Springfield, NJ 07081   Hants GU12 6BP
USA   UK

http://www.enslow.com

Library of Congress Cataloging-in-Publication Data

Cole, Michael D.
    The L.A. Riots : rage in the City of Angels / Michael D. Cole.
        p. cm. — (American disasters)
    Includes bibliographical references and index.
    Summary: Discusses the riots that occurred in Los Angeles in 1992
after the verdict in the Rodney King case.
    ISBN 0-7660-1219-0
    1. Los Angeles (Calif.)—Race Relations—Juvenile literature.
2. Riots—California—Los Angeles—History—20th century—Juvenile
literature. 3. Violence—California—Los Angeles—History—20th
century—Juvenile literature. 4. Racism—California—Los Angeles—
Juvenile literature. 5. King, Rodney—Juvenile literature.
[1. Riots—California—Los Angeles. 2. Los Angeles (Calif.)—Race
relations. 3. Race relations.] I. Title. II. Series.
F869.L89A252   1999
979.4'94053—dc21   98-30263
                                                                  CIP
                                                                  AC

Printed in the United States of America

10 9 8 7 6 5 4 3 2 1

To Our Readers:
All Internet addresses in this book were active and appropriate when we went
to press. Any comments or suggestions can be sent by e-mail to
Comments@enslow.com or to the address on the back cover.

Illustration Credits: AP/Wide World Photos, pp. 1, 6, 8, 10, 12, 14, 16, 18, 21,
24, 25, 26, 28, 29, 31, 33, 36, 37, 40, 43.

Cover Illustration: AP/Wide World Photos

Contents

CHAPTER 1

A City in Rage

Choi Sai-Choi was a Chinese immigrant living in Los Angeles, California. He was driving his car through the south-central section of the city late in the afternoon of April 29, 1992. He did not know the city, whose name in Spanish means "the city of angels," was about to erupt in violence.

Choi slowed his car down as he got near the intersection of Florence and Normandie streets. A small crowd of people were waving their hands.

"I was afraid I may [sic] bump into them," Choi later said. But within moments his concern for the others turned into fear for his own safety. The group, consisting of African-American men, gathered around his car. They began hitting the doors and windows and shouting furiously at Choi.

"People rushed toward my car and tried to open my door," he said. "I took hold of the keys with my hand, then I was being pulled out by those people from my car."[1]

Choi was pulled from his car and badly beaten by this

rioting group of men. His head and lower back were badly injured in the incident, and Choi was left bleeding and helpless.

A short time later, an off-duty Los Angeles firefighter came to his rescue. Donald R. Jones, another African American, helped Choi back into his car. Choi was grateful that Jones had come to help him.

"When I walked over to him," Jones said, "he clutched both my legs with his arms and said, 'Thank you.'"[2]

The intersection of Florence and Normandie streets in South-Central Los Angeles where Choi Sai-Choi and, later, Reginald Denny were beaten.

It was ironic that an African-American man was helping a beaten Chinese immigrant on this occasion. Acts of destruction and violence, motivated by racial tensions, were occurring all over South-Central Los Angeles that afternoon.

A short time later, a white truck driver named Reginald Denny drove toward the same intersection at Florence and Normandie streets. Traffic was stopped. Some cars had been abandoned in the streets. Denny could not get through in his truck.

As a news helicopter flew overhead, videotaping the event, a number of young African-American men ran toward Denny's truck. The men got inside the truck's cab and pulled Denny out onto the street. Once Denny was on the street, they surrounded him and began to kick and beat him savagely. While Denny was already down and bleeding, one of the attackers threw a cinder block at his head. When the block struck Denny, the attacker threw up his arms and did a dance of celebration.[3]

Such images were frightening to watch. The videotape of this and other attacks that were taking place in this Southern California city on April 29, 1992, were broadcast over and over on television news programs around the world. The pictures told a terrible story—South-Central Los Angeles had gone mad.

A disturbing videotape of another beating, one that had taken place more than a year earlier, had started it all. That videotape was taken in March 1991. It showed a group of white police officers beating an African-American

*R*eginald Denny became the national symbol of the hundreds of riot victims. In this 1989 photo he is pictured with his daughter Ashley.

suspect. The suspect's name was Rodney King. The Rodney King incident had stirred the city's already delicate racial tensions. Now, a year later, the chain of events that the Rodney King beating had set off was causing a disaster.

CHAPTER 2

Shocking Images

Rodney King was a twenty-five-year-old unemployed construction worker. He was out on parole after serving a term in prison for armed robbery. Shortly after midnight on March 3, 1991, a California Highway Patrol unit spotted King's car speeding down San Fernando's Foothill freeway at more than one hundred miles per hour. The patrol unit began to chase King and the two passengers in his speeding car.

When King exited the freeway, officers from the Los Angeles Police Department (L.A.P.D.) joined the chase. His car was finally stopped in an area of the city called Lake View Terrace. The officers ordered King to get out of his car, which he did, reluctantly. Four officers tried to subdue him, but King, who was a big man, threw all of them off. When King refused to be handcuffed, Sergeant Stacey Koon hit him with two Tazer darts. These are designed to stun or subdue violent suspects. Instead, King lunged at the officers.[1]

Rodney King was repeatedly beaten by Los Angeles police in March 1991.

Because King did not appear to be quieted by the Tazer darts, the officers feared that he might be under the influence of a drug called PCP.[2] This harmful drug has been known to give people extra strength for a short time. Together, the officers managed to get King to the ground. Once he was down, three of the officers began to beat him with their police batons. The fourth officer, Stacey Koon, did nothing to try to stop them. King was still moving, but he did not get up. The officers continued the beating. They did not know that they were being videotaped.

A local resident, George Holliday, had heard all the noise outside his apartment. He had grabbed his video camera and was recording the beating.

"The sirens and copter noise woke me up," Holliday's wife said later. "I went out on the balcony and saw all the commotion and called George." She told Holliday, "Maybe you should get the new camera. There is a lot going on out there."

"I found the camera," Holliday said. "It took a little

time to get it ready and for me to start shooting. I just followed the action."[3]

The action Holliday followed was the continued beating of Rodney King by three of the four white officers. King had behaved in a threatening manner and had resisted arrest. But the videotape captured images of the officers kicking and beating King with their batons, even after he appeared to be subdued.

Despite the fact that King had fled from police in his car at a very dangerous speed, had resisted arrest, and had threatened the officers trying to arrest him, his beating, recorded on the videotape, appeared to be excessive. The images of the three officers beating King, while a fourth officer watched, were shocking.

The tape was turned over to KTLA, a Los Angeles television station. It was shown during one of KTLA's newscasts. Only a few seconds of King's own aggressive behavior leading up to the beating were recorded on the tape. The tape mostly showed the scene of the three officers repeatedly beating King while he was already on the ground. Within hours, the tape was shown on all the major television networks.

The shocking images of Los Angeles police officers repeatedly beating a suspect were seen by people around the world. People were outraged. The L.A.P.D. and Los Angeles mayor Tom Bradley were immediately under attack from the media and the angry citizens of Los Angeles. The tape showed that King was kicked or clubbed a total of fifty-six times in eighty-one seconds.

*L*os Angeles mayor Tom Bradley came under sharp criticism for the Rodney King beating, along with the L.A.P.D.

The Rodney King incident outraged many people. However, it was only one of several factors leading to the Los Angeles riots a year later. The people of South-Central Los Angeles were already plagued by many problems before this videotaped beating had ever occurred.

South-Central Los Angeles was poor. It was home to a large number of African Americans, Hispanics, and Asian Americans. Many companies and factories had left the area. Their departure left many people out of work. With so few jobs, many young men became members of street gangs and got involved in crime. Drug use was on the rise. There was also resentment among some African

Americans and Hispanics over the number of businesses in the area owned by Koreans. This collection of problems caused tensions to build among the ethnic groups living within the south-central district.

These racial and economic problems created a very difficult situation for the police. As in many other large United States cities, there was a strained relationship between the police and minorities. It was difficult to maintain order in an area like South-Central Los Angeles without using some amount of force. Yet the use of force during arrests in the crime-stricken neighborhood led to the belief that police brutality was too easily used against minorities. Such a belief created a great mistrust of the police department.[4]

This was the environment in which the videotaped beating of Rodney King emerged. The images on the tape seemed to confirm what many people in that poor section of the city already believed—that the police were brutalizing suspects. The fact that the four police officers involved were white and Rodney King was African-American only heightened an already bad situation.

It would get even worse.

Police officers Stacey Koon, Laurence Powell, Theodore Briseno, and Timothy Wind were charged with assault in the Rodney King incident. Months later, in November 1991, it was announced that their trial would be moved to Simi Valley, a city just outside Los Angeles. The trial was moved because attorneys argued that the publicity surrounding the case would make it difficult to conduct a fair trial within Los Angeles itself.

The trouble was that Simi Valley was a mostly white neighborhood. It was also home to a large number of police officers and firefighters. A twelve-member jury was selected for the trial. It included ten whites, one Hispanic, and one Filipino. Protests followed when it was learned that not one African American was selected for the jury.

*T*his mural in downtown San Francisco showed the four defendants in the Rodney King civil rights trial. The words on the wall read, "White men can jump if you are willing to pay for it."

Some of the jurors had even been security guards or had relatives in the L.A.P.D.

Considering the racially sensitive nature of the case, the ethnic makeup of the jury was not well balanced. It seemed that the citizens chosen for the jury were all more likely to identify with the police officers than with their victim, Rodney King. To many people, especially those in South-Central Los Angeles, it did not appear that the trial was being run fairly.

The Rodney King case was not the only case angering minorities in South-Central Los Angeles. Just two weeks after the King beating, a Korean-American grocery store owner named Soon Ja Do had shot and killed a fifteen-year-old African-American girl. Soon claimed the girl was trying to rob a bottle of orange juice from her store. The shooting was captured on a security camera videotape. A jury convicted Soon of voluntary manslaughter. She faced the possibility of serving eleven years in prison. However, the judge later sentenced Soon to only five years of probation and a five-hundred-dollar fine. To some, it seemed that Soon had received an extremely light sentence for shooting a young girl to death.[5]

The fact that the girl was an African American and Soon was a Korean American deepened racial anger in the community. It seemed that the justice system had sided with the Korean American against the African American. This happened only eleven days before the Rodney King trial was moved to the mostly white town of Simi Valley.

During the trial of the L.A.P.D. officers, the jury

viewed the videotaped beating frame by frame. Lawyers for the police officers argued that the blows to King were necessary to subdue him. The jury members viewed the entire tape. The beginning showed King lunging aggressively at the officers. This part of the tape had never been shown on television. Seeing the part of the tape in which King acted aggressively may have caused the jury members to view the officers' actions in a new light.

The trial ended, and the verdict came on the afternoon of April 29, 1992. The jury found the four officers not guilty of any acts of assault against Rodney King. The jurors were undecided on one count of excessive force

*J*udge Stanley Weisberg presided over the Rodney King beating trial in Simi Valley.

against officer Laurence Powell, so the judge declared a mistrial on that count.

The verdicts shocked the people of Los Angeles, both minorities and whites.

One African-American man from South-Central Los Angeles said the police officers "should have gotten at least six months. It's not fair." He also compared the verdict with the earlier case of Soon Ja Do. "They've been beating us for months. What's right is right. People can't keep living like this. People are tired of this."[6]

"I just couldn't believe what I was hearing," said one woman. "To arrest a man is one thing, but to beat him with four or five people, with their guns drawn? I was just shocked."[7]

"I'm not only shocked," said Rose Brown, a Los Angeles woman who had driven to Simi Valley to hear the verdicts, "I'm hurt for Americans as a people . . . I don't think Rodney King was on trial, but I think America was on trial."[8]

In the aftermath of the verdicts, Brown could sense the tension building in the City of Angels throughout the afternoon.

CHAPTER 3

Riot!

It was wrong!" yelled Tonia Smith at the intersection of 55th and Normandie streets in South-Central Los Angeles. "They beat that black man [Rodney King]. It's time for us black folks . . . to reunite!"

At the same intersection, a cardboard sign in the middle of the street read, "Black men and women are fair game for shooting and beating at the hands of L.A.P.D."[1]

Hours after the verdict in the Rodney King case was delivered on Wednesday, April 29, 1992, a crowd was beginning to gather nearby at the intersection of Florence and Normandie streets. As dusk approached, the mood of the crowd turned ugly. Starting at about 5:30 P.M., some people in the crowd began to throw rocks and bottles at passing cars. A nearby store was then broken into and looted. It was at this time that Choi Sai-Choi, the Chinese immigrant, became one of the first victims of the riots.

Police officers tried to control the worsening situation at Florence and Normandie streets, but they were forced

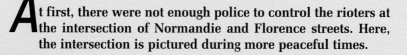

to withdraw. The angry mob was beginning to present a serious threat to the officers.

"We didn't have enough numbers to go in," said Commander Robert Gil, a police spokesman. "You can't go in if you have only four or five officers. You have to have a sufficient number."[2]

At first, there were not enough police to control the rioters at the intersection of Normandie and Florence streets. Here, the intersection is pictured during more peaceful times.

Crowds were getting out of control elsewhere, too. At the corner of 71st and Normandie streets, a crowd became violent as police attempted to make arrests. The officers pulled out their batons when rocks and bottles were thrown at their patrol cars. After struggling for several minutes, the sergeant got on a loudspeaker and told the officers, "It's not worth it, let's get out of here."

"They shouldn't never [sic] have left," said a twenty-year-old African-American resident. The young man, named E.J., said the mob surrounded the cars of people "who were light-skinned or white." One man who tried to take pictures of the scene had his camera stolen and was brutally attacked.

"He just barely got away," E.J. said. "If some black guy hadn't helped him, he probably would be dead right now."

E.J. then saw a white woman driving her van with children in the back. "I told her, 'Get out of the neighborhood, you better get out of here—look at all these people.'"[3]

In another neighborhood, eighteen-year-old Carlos Mejía did not get out in time. Mejía was on his way to pick up his cousin from work when a mob surrounded his car.

"Five came from one side, and five came from the other," Mejía said. "They asked me if I was white and then they started throwing bricks at the car." One of the bricks smashed through Mejía's windshield and hit him in the head. Within moments there was so much blood coming from the wound in his head that Mejía could barely see to drive. But he kept going, trying to get away.

"I thought if I stopped, they would kill me," he said. Fortunately, Mejía got away.[4]

It was about 6:30 P.M. when Reginald Denny drove his truck into the intersection of Florence and Normandie streets. A helicopter flying overhead taped the scene as Denny was dragged from his truck and beaten by a group of rioters.

"We were watching TV at home," said T.J. Murphy, who was watching Denny's beating with a woman friend, Terri Barnett. "'Somebody's got to get that guy out of there,' we said to each other."[5]

The images on television caused Murphy and Barnett to get in their car to see what trouble was happening around them. They didn't know they would end up help-ing rescue Denny. When they arrived at the intersection of Florence and Normandie streets, the police were nowhere to be seen.

Someone had helped Denny get back into his truck, and now he was trying to get it out of the intersection. But Denny's face was covered with blood, and his eyes were swollen shut. A young woman was standing on the side of the truck, giving directions to the blinded Denny. As the truck moved along an inch at a time, she would tell him to turn the steering wheel to the right or the left.

Then Murphy and Barnett saw another young African-American man jump into the cab. In the violent confusion of the day, Murphy and Barnett feared that the man might be another rioter trying to finish Denny off. Instead, the man pushed Denny across the seat and took over driving

*F*rom right to back: Lei Yuille, Terri Barnett, T.J. Murphy, and Gregory Alan Williams all helped rescue Denny from his attackers.

the truck. The woman also crawled inside the cab to take care of Denny.

Murphy then jumped up on the side of the truck to assist the new driver, who could not see through the truck's shattered windshield. Barnett cleared the way for the truck by driving her car ahead of them with the hazard lights blinking.

"You're going to make it," the woman in the cab told Denny. "You're going to be OK."[6]

After a difficult drive through the city streets, the truck pulled up to the emergency room at Daniel Freeman Hospital. Paramedics frantically worked on Denny until he was rushed to surgery.

"One more minute, just one more minute," one of the paramedics said, "and he would have been dead."[7]

The response of these African Americans to help Denny, a white man, showed that human courage and compassion existed amid the madness of the riots. Not everyone in South-Central Los Angeles was rioting.

Most of the more violent acts were being committed by gang members who had had a history of violence and crime before the riots ever began. The group of men who attacked Reginald Denny were all members of a gang called the Eight Trey Gangster Crips.[8] Many gang members were using the riot as an excuse to commit crimes. They justified their actions by claiming to avenge the injustice

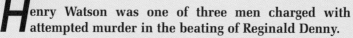
Henry Watson was one of three men charged with attempted murder in the beating of Reginald Denny.

*M*embers of rival L.A. street gangs met later to work toward a mutual understanding.

to Rodney King. In the cause of spreading violence and destruction, the gangs were unified.

Even as police approached, one young gang member would not move.

"We ain't afraid of them [the police]," he said. "We got guns just like them. Go on, harass me!" he yelled to the police. "You know that verdict wasn't right. . . . Are you going to beat me like Rodney King? Come on. Just try it."[9]

Although gang members were responsible for many of the more violent acts, other people were taking part in the riots in other ways. Some drivers blared their horns and yelled out their windows. Others began to ignore the traffic lights. Fires were started in trash barrels and pushed into the street. It was a carnival-like atmosphere that began to turn ugly as one store after another was broken into and looted. People were breaking into markets and stealing armloads of groceries.[10]

"Free food! Free food!" they shouted as they fled the store with their stolen goods. Many others who had been standing around watching could not resist the temptation to join in. "People are running, dropping everything," said one boy. "I feel like this is a dream or something."[11]

By nightfall, the fires that at first had been started only in trash Dumpsters were being started inside shops and other buildings. Within a few hours, smoke was rising from burning buildings all over South-Central Los Angeles. The intersection of Florence and Normandie streets was now in ruins. Every store and business at the intersection had been broken into and burned, except for a gas station that was already boarded up.

The Los Angeles Fire Department was quickly overwhelmed with alarms. While firefighters risked their lives to battle the flames, some of them had the added danger of snipers taking shots at them. As violence and looting continued to spread through the city, reports of fires were received in record numbers.

"They're coming in about one a minute," said a Fire Department spokesman. "And I think it's going to go on like that all night."[12]

Every few moments, shooting could be heard in the streets. Groups of rioters continued to beat innocent people, some of them to death. The fires that were set began to take on a pattern. It appeared that some African-American and Hispanic rioters were targeting Korean businesses. Before the day was done, some Korean business owners were carrying guns to defend themselves and their stores from being looted and burned.

A state of violent chaos was spreading through the city.

Los Angeles firefighters were quickly overwhelmed with a wave of new blazes and the growing danger of being hit by sniper fire.

*S*ome Korean store owners, like Joon Ho Lee, above, used guns to protect their stores and themselves from angry rioters and looters.

At shortly after 9 P.M., barely seven hours after the Rodney King verdict had been announced, Los Angeles mayor Tom Bradley declared a state of emergency. A few minutes later, California governor Pete Wilson ordered the National Guard to report for duty. The chaos continued into the night; Mayor Bradley went on television just after 11 P.M. to address the city.

"Stay off the streets. It's anticipated that a curfew will be put into effect tomorrow night," Bradley said, assuring citizens that the authorities would "take whatever resources [were] needed" to stop the riots.

"We believe that the situation is now simmering down," Bradley added, "[It's] pretty much under control."[13]

But he was wrong. The worst was yet to come.

CHAPTER 4

Red Blood, Black Smoke

By the end of the first night of rioting, more than one hundred fifty buildings in the city were smoking ruins. Many others were still burning. Countless businesses had been broken into and looted. At least ten people were dead as a result of the riots. Dozens more were seriously injured.

However, the dawning of April 30, 1992, did not bring calm to the city.

In fact, the trouble was spreading. Soon the fires, looting, and robberies spread to the mostly white communities of Westwood, Hollywood, and Beverly Hills. The police had lost control of the situation, and the rioters seemed to know it.

Los Angeles police chief Daryl Gates, a white, had been sharply criticized throughout the trial of the four officers involved in the Rodney King beating. Many accused Gates and his department of having racist attitudes and allowing police brutality against minorities.

Yet it appeared that even Gates and his department were caught unprepared for the reaction to the trial's shocking verdict. They were not ready for the violence it ignited in the city.

Gates was at a fundraising event when the riots started. He was slow to call off-duty officers back to work. However, it is doubtful that the police could have stopped the riots, even if they had been better prepared with more officers on the streets. Still, without enough police on duty, the

Critics accused Police Chief Daryl Gates of failing to discourage police brutality and racism within the L.A.P.D.

level of unrest during the riot's first night was allowed to worsen. After nightfall, the police department's control of the city had deteriorated rapidly.[1]

In the early morning hours of Thursday, April 30, the rioting continued to intensify. Amid mounting criticism from the media and the public, Gates admitted that his officers were greatly overwhelmed by the scope of the riots. National Guard troops were on their way, but it would be hours before they would arrive to assist the police and sheriff's deputies.

In the meantime, police rode with firefighters to

protect them from sniper gunfire and the interference of angry mobs. As fires raged on one side of a street, whole families would participate in looting retail businesses and grocery stores on the other side.

"There were even little kids running in for their parents," said a shocked store owner. "'Go on in, run in and get more,'" he said the parents told their children.[2]

"You had seven- and eight-year-olds all the way up to sixty-year-olds," said a woman watching the riots. "You had everyday citizens. . . . I thought about participating myself."[3]

"It's kids . . . women with children," said another owner as he guarded his store. "We can't call the cops. We can't call anyone. You're on your own. Is there ever going to be an end to this?"[4]

"Everybody else is grabbing and taking what they can take," said a young woman outside another store. "Why not me? This ain't stealing. Ain't nobody [sic] in the store. It's free now."[5]

Gang members shot at police, firefighters, and passing motorists. One man on a motorcycle was yanked off and beaten by a mob of fifteen young men before one pulled a gun and shot the motorcyclist in the back of the head.

In the terrible hours before the National Guard troops arrived, Mayor Tom Bradley addressed the city on television once more. He described how in the aftermath of the verdict, the rioters "chose the opportunity to steal, loot, vandalize and, indeed, to kill." He added, "That, we cannot—and we will not—tolerate."[6]

Many businesses were crippled during the riots when looters took advantage of the chaos and stole merchandise from unoccupied shops.

National Guard troops began arriving late in the afternoon. There had been delays in organizing their assignments and getting the ammunition for their guns. When they finally began to move in, they were met by jeers from rioters. Angry graffiti messages painted by gang members were everywhere. Many of the messages were directed at the arriving troops.

The most violent rioters had clearly begun to fear no one. Many gang members flashed their guns and cursed at the troops. Some yelled at the troops to get out or risk being killed.

A group of National Guard military policemen headed toward the corner of Vernon and Figueroa streets. They were going there to relieve a group of police officers and sheriff's deputies. There was a struggle to contain the violence at that location. Cars were overturned and burned. Trash and broken glass were everywhere. Some of the rioters were carrying guns.

When the guardsmen arrived at the corner of Vernon and Figueroa streets, the crowd yelled at them and threatened them. Other rioters continued to loot a store across the street. Then suddenly one of them, a gang member, ran up to one of the guardsmen. The gang member tried to take the guardsman's M-16 rifle away from him. The two men struggled over the weapon for a few moments. Then another soldier saw what was happening. The soldier stepped over and swiftly knocked the gang member in the head with the butt of his own rifle. The gang member crumpled to the pavement. His friends quickly grabbed him and carried him away.

The incident with the gang member caused the rioters to think twice about threatening the soldiers anymore. The crowd gradually faded away from the intersection.[7]

The soldiers had managed to restore order in that part of the city. But other areas raged on into a second night of rioting. Mayor Bradley put a dusk-to-dawn curfew into effect for the entire city. Police officers, sheriff's deputies, firefighters, and National Guard units still could not keep up with the reports of looting and arson. The original

Armed federal troops were called in to protect Los Angeles when the rioting became too widespread.

*R*odney King is shown here on his way to the press conference where he would make his famous plea for unity, "Can we all get along?"

request for two thousand National Guard soldiers was increased to six thousand on Thursday night.

Community leaders and church pastors went out into the streets to plead with the rioters to stop. Unfortunately, most crowds were in no mood to listen.

Even Rodney King himself urged the rioters to bring the madness to an end. "People, I just want to say. . . can we all get along?" King pleaded in a publicly televised statement. "I mean we're all stuck here for a while. Let's try to work it out."[8]

To help end the violence, President George Bush ordered forty-five hundred federal troops into the city. This assistance came at the request of Mayor Bradley. He felt the National Guard troops should have been put in place more quickly.[9]

Dawn on Friday, May 1, revealed a city shrouded in smoke. After the second night of rioting, forty people were dead. More than eighteen hundred were injured. Fires continued to burn, but the number of emergency calls was gradually beginning to decrease.[10]

Throughout Friday, troops continued to take up positions in riot-torn areas of the city. The tide slowly turned. However, many areas of the city, especially South-Central Los Angeles, had already been ravaged. People who lived in those parts of the city, but had not taken part in the riots, were deeply upset and frustrated.

"I cried last night, and I cried this morning when I saw what they had done," said Carol Clark, the manager of a ravaged Thrifty pharmacy. "This was just an opportunity to loot, and people took advantage of it."[11]

The anger and resentment many African Americans and Hispanics felt toward Koreans in their communities, because the Koreans owned so many businesses, had caused Korean-owned businesses to be hit especially hard. Many of their businesses were looted and burned.

This attitude toward the Koreans certainly was not held by all African Americans or Hispanics in their communities. When cleanup efforts began, people of all ethnic backgrounds and races helped each other.

"I especially wanted to help the Koreans," said one African-American volunteer. "I don't want them to think so negatively about blacks. The violence last night wasn't real. This is real."[12]

People's frustration over the self-destruction of their neighborhoods was widespread.

"It's really out of control," said one man. "I mean, I'm Hispanic and we're killing our own. It's ridiculous, man."

"This is not unity," said another young man. "This is destroying. This is like getting angry and setting your own house on fire."[13]

"Right now they're bringing down the place," added Carol Clark about her looted Thrifty pharmacy. "But two days from now, when they're laughing and their mom sends them out to get milk, they're going to think: Where?"[14]

The riots gradually came to an end as federal troops dispersed throughout the city on Saturday afternoon. Eventually, the fires were all put out, and the smoke began to clear over the wounded city.

The riots were over.

As the situation in Los Angeles slowly returned to normal, the rioters found themselves living amid the destruction they had caused. In four days of rioting, they had reduced many communities to a landscape of ruined buildings and broken lives.

A situation that had already been difficult for many people was now much worse.

CHAPTER 5

Grim Lessons

The Los Angeles riots of 1992 were the worst riots in United States history. Sixty people were killed. More than twenty-three hundred were injured. Nearly ten thousand businesses were looted and burned.[1]

In areas where many people were already poor or without work, it was now even more difficult to find jobs or a place to buy groceries. The places where people had shopped or gone to work had been destroyed. Economic problems deepened, and so did the tension between ethnic groups in the community. Unity seemed impossible.

A group called Rebuild L.A. was organized to lead efforts in reconstructing the areas stricken by the riots. This group met with many problems. It had trouble finding banks and investors interested in helping. Few wished to take the risk of investing their money to rebuild shops and start new businesses in the damaged communities. Investors feared that riots and violence might destroy the businesses all over again.

There were many other aftereffects. Mayor Tom Bradley's popularity plunged following the riots. He did not seek a sixth term of office. Police Chief Daryl Gates was sharply criticized for his department's slow response to the riots. He later retired from his position. He was replaced by Willie Williams, an African American. Williams promised that his department would improve relations between citizens and the police.

Troubles for the police officers involved in the Rodney King beating were also not over. Although they had been

Korean Americans, African Americans, Latinos, and whites join in a peace march through the Koreatown area of Los Angeles. An estimated twenty-five thousand people called for peace and unity in the city.

found not guilty of criminal assault during the beating, the United States Justice Department conducted an investigation to determine whether the four officers had violated King's civil rights. A trial was later held in a federal district court. On April 17, 1993, the federal jury convicted officers Stacey Koon and Laurence Powell of violating King's civil rights, by harming him while he was under arrest. Officers Timothy Wind and Theodore Briseno were acquitted of all charges. On August 4, 1993, Stacey Koon and Laurence Powell were sentenced to thirty months in a federal prison.[2]

In the mid-1990s, economic problems in California made efforts at recovery even more difficult. Continued violence between gangs also turned many investors away from the riot-damaged communities. Despite the many problems, some people in the stricken areas were making an effort to heal the wounds. James Shackelford owned a construction company. He tried to lure young men away from gangs by employing them in his company.

"You are the young men we have, whether the world likes it or not, whether we like it or not," he said to them. "You guys are our future; we have to depend on it."[3]

Despite the city's turmoils, some believed that Los Angeles could get beyond its many problems.

"Everyone wants to get beyond the King beating and the [Reginald] Denny beating," wrote author Kevin Starr. Starr believed that the city had all the basic economic tools necessary to make a "stunning economic recovery, if it can mend its social differences."[4]

Mending those social differences would be a slow and difficult task. It takes years, even generations, to rebuild communities and establish a sense of trust among people of different backgrounds.

In addition, relations between minorities and the police in Los Angeles never seemed to improve significantly. That relationship was damaged once again during the highly publicized murder trial of O. J. Simpson in 1995. In that trial, Simpson was accused of murdering his ex-wife, Nicole Brown Simpson, and her friend Ronald Goldman.

Simpson was an African American and most of the detectives involved in investigating the murder were white. During the trial, Simpson's attorneys argued that the murder investigation was carried out by racist L.A.P.D. detectives. They were accused of tampering with evidence in an effort to frame Simpson. One of the detectives, Mark Fuhrman, had been recorded on tape making a number of racist remarks. His comments seemed to show he had mistreated African Americans while he was on duty.

The strategy of accusing the L.A.P.D. of racism turned the tide in the trial. Simpson was found not guilty of the murders. Once again the relationship between the L.A.P.D. and minorities in Los Angeles had been dealt a damaging blow.

The timing of the verdict in the Simpson trial showed that the L.A.P.D. had learned at least one important lesson from the riots. After the Simpson jury returned its decision, it was decided to delay the public announcement until 10 A.M. the next morning.

"At 10 A.M. you have the morning watch on duty and the day watch coming on, along with detectives," said Dennis Zine of the Los Angeles Police Protective League. "This gives the police enough uniformed officers to respond to any hot spots that could develop."[5]

The way to announce racially sensitive trial verdicts in the city had been decided months earlier. The strategy was the result of a grim lesson learned the hard way.

Little good came from the destruction and violence that occurred during the Los Angeles riots. They had been a tragedy of human failings. They showed everyone the terrible cost of our human imperfections and racial misunderstandings. Today, only time and renewed efforts to understand and respect our cultural differences can heal the scars of this critical disaster.

*P*edestrians along Vermont Street pass under a fast food restaurant sign, which displays an optimistic message about L.A.'s future.

Chapter 1. A City in Rage

1. Robert Garcia, *Riots and Rebellion* (CD-ROM), Stanford University, 1997.

2. Ibid.

3. Laurie Becklund and Stephanie Chavez, "Beaten Driver a Searing Image of Mob Cruelty," *The Los Angeles Times*, May 1, 1992,<http://www.latimes.com/HOME/NEWS/REPORTS/RIOTS/0501dnny.htm> (June 30, 1998).

Chapter 2. Shocking Images

1. James D. Delk, *Fires and Furies: The L.A. Riots: What Really Happened.* (Palm Springs, Calif.; ETC Publications, 1995), p. 17.

2. Stan Chambers, "Rodney King and the Los Angeles Riots," CitiVU homepage, 1997.

3. Ibid.

4. John Salak, *The Los Angeles Riots: America's Cities in Crisis* (Brookfield, Conn., Millbrook Press, 1993), pp. 23–26.

5. Robert Garcia, *Riots and Rebellion* (CD-ROM), Stanford University, 1997.

6. Marc Lacey and Shawn Hubler, "Rioters Set Fires, Loot Stores; 4 Reported Dead," *The Los Angeles Times*, April 30, 1992,<http://www.latimes.com/HOME/NEWS/REPORTS/RIOTS/0430loot.htm> (June 30, 1998).

7. Amy Wallace and David Ferrell, "Verdicts Greeted With Outrage and Disbelief," *The Los Angeles Times*, April 30, 1992, <http://www.latimes.com/HOME/NEWS/REPORTS/RIOTS/0430reax.htm> (June 30, 1998).

8. Ibid.

Chapter 3. Riot!

1. Amy Wallace and David Ferrell, "Verdicts Greeted With Outrage and Disbelief," *The Los Angeles Times*, April 30, 1992, <http://www.latimes.com/HOME/NEWS/REPORTS/RIOTS/0430reax.htm> (June 30, 1998).

2. Marc Lacey and Shawn Hubler, "Rioters Set Fires, Loot Stores; 4 Reported Dead," *The Los Angeles Times*, April 30, 1992, <http://www.latimes.com/HOME/NEWS/REPORTS/RIOTS/0430loot.htm> (June 30, 1998).

3. Ibid.

4. Charisse Jones and Dean E. Murphy, "A Long Night of Anger, Anarchy," *The Los Angeles Times*, May 1, 1992, <http://www.latimes.com/HOME/NEWS/REPORTS/RIOTS/0501good.htm> (June 30, 1998).

5. Laurie Becklund and Stephanie Chavez, "Beaten Driver a Searing Image of Mob Cruelty," *The Los Angeles Times*, May 1, 1992,<http://www.latimes.com/HOME/NEWS/REPORTS/RIOTS/0501dnny.htm> (June 30, 1998).

6. Ibid.

7. Ibid.

8. James D. Delk, *Fires and Furies: The L.A. Riots: What Really Happened.* (Palm Springs, Calif.: ETC Publications, 1995), p. 279.

9. Jones and Murphy.

10. Delk, pp. 30–31.

11. Jones and Murphy.

12. Lacey and Hubler.

13. Ibid.

Chapter 4. Red Blood, Black Smoke

1. John Salak, *The Los Angeles Riots: America's Cities in Crisis* (Brookfield, Conn., Millbrook Press, 1993), pp. 23–26.

2. Greg Braxton and Jim Newton, "Looting and Fires Ravage L.A." *The Los Angeles Times,* May 1, 1992, <http://www.latimes.com/HOME/NEWS/REPORTS/RIOTS/0501lede.htm> (June 30, 1998).

3. Victor Merina and John Mitchell, "Opportunists, Criminals Get Blame for Riots," *The Los Angeles Times,* May 1, 1992, <http://www.latimes.com/HOME/NEWS/REPORTS/RIOTS/0501blam.htm> (June 30, 1998).

4. Braxton and Newton.

5. Merina and Mitchell.

6. Braxton and Newton.

7. James D. Delk, *Fires and Furies: The L.A. Riots: What Really Happened* (Palm Springs, Calif.: ETC Publications, 1995), p. 64.

8. Salak, p. 39.

9. Delk, pp. 98–100.

10. Ibid., pp. 154–155.

11. Braxton and Newton.

12. Paul Lieberman and Dean E. Murphy, "Bush Ordering Troops to L.A." *The Los Angeles Times,* May 2, 1992, <http://www. latimes.com/HOME/NEWS/REPORTS/RIOTS/0502lede.htm> (June 30, 1998).

13. Merina and Mitchell.

14. Braxton and Newton.

Chapter 5. Grim Lessons

1. Lou Cannon, "A Year After Riots, 'Lotus Land' Seeks to Shed Badlands Image," *The Washington Post,* April 30, 1993, <http://www.washingtonpost.com/wp-srv/national/longterm/lariots/stories/1year.htm> (June 30, 1998).

2. James D. Delk, *Fires and Furies: The L.A. Riots: What Really Happened* (Palm Springs, Calif.: ETC Publications, 1995), p. 315.

3. Cannon.

4. Ibid.

5. Michael Hedges, "The Delay: Los Angeles Learns from Rodney King Verdict," *The Detroit News,* October 3, 1995, <http://detnews.com/menu/stories/18732.htm> (June 30, 1998).

acquittal—Setting someone free from the charge of an offense or crime.

arson—The purposeful act of setting a structure on fire. Arson may be committed simply as an act of destruction or as an act of fraud by a person who sets fire to his own property in order to collect illegally the insurance money on that property.

attorney—A legally qualified person whose job it is to represent and carry out the wishes of another person in legal matters.

curfew—A rule that orders citizens to leave the streets and close businesses at a specified time. Curfews are usually applied only in emergencies, such as during wartime or riots. Curfews are sometimes specific to young people and are used to keep them off the streets at night.

looting—Large-scale acts of stealing and robbing, usually in times of war, riot, or natural disaster.

mistrial—A trial that, at its end, has no legal effect due to some serious error or mistake in the conduct of the trial itself.

probation—The period during which a person is free although found guilty of a crime. However, during this period the guilty person's behavior is periodically monitored and evaluated by a probation officer.

Further Reading

Books

Alan-Williams, Gregory. *A Gathering of Heroes—Reflections on Rage and Responsibility: A Memoir of the Los Angeles Riots.* Chicago: Academy Chicago Publishers, 1994.

Delk, James D. *Fires and Furies: The L.A. Riots: What Really Happened?* Palm Springs, Calif.: ETC Publications, 1995.

Hamilton, Sue L. *Los Angeles Riots: The Day of the Disaster.* Minneapolis: Abdo and Daughters, 1992.

Salak, John. *The Los Angeles Riots: America's Cities in Crisis.* Brookfield, Conn.: The Millbrook Press, 1993.

Internet

"L.A. Riots: Five Years Later." *The Washington Post* <http://www.washingtonpost.com/wp-srv/national/longterm/lariots/lariots.htm (July 31, 1998).

The Los Angeles Times. <http://www.latimes.com/HOME/ NEWS/REPORTS/RIOTS/> (June 30, 1998).